I Wanted To Dance With My Father

poems by

Jan Ball

Finishing Line Press
Georgetown, Kentucky

I Wanted To Dance With My Father

ACKNOWLEDGMENTS

I wanted to dance with my father, *Calyx*
Grandma Doll, *Iodine Poetry Review*
objects from childhood, *The South Carolina Review*
Stems, *Roanoke Review*
where the water lilies grow, *Up and Under*
Ozark Vacation, *Miller's Pond*
my dad makes polish sausage, *Tapestries*
bacon fat, *By & By*
circus flower, *Faircloth Review*
burying my sister, *Potomac Review*
aunties, *Ostentatious Mind*
Restless Night, *Sanskrit Literary Arts Magazine*
chagall playground, *Nth Position* (England)
my father's boxy girl, *Verse Wisconsin*
bad girl, *California Quarterly*
fruit basket, *Plain Spoke*
better than throwing stones, *Presa*
Mrs. Johnson's Trading Card Collection, *Plain Spoke*
Suspended for Smoking, *Indiana Voice Journal*
vocation, *Fulcrum*

Publisher: Leah Maines
Editor: Christen Kincaid
Cover Art: Quentin Ball
Author Photo: Quentin Ball
Cover Design: Elizabeth Maines McCleavy

Printed in the USA on acid-free paper.
Order online: www.finishinglinepress.com
also available on amazon.com

Author inquiries and mail orders:
Finishing Line Press
P. O. Box 1626
Georgetown, Kentucky 40324
U. S. A.

Table of Contents

The greater the storm,
the brighter the rainbow

I wanted to dance with my father

I wanted to dance with my father, to glide
around the floor in my patent-leather shoes
with my blue skirt and crinolines whirling
like sails as my dad maneuvered me
between the other smiling Polish couples
at the wedding like a captain propelling
a ship through a sparkling sea, intimately
sensitive to every landmark, the hall still
smelling briny of sauerkraut and roast beef.
Swirling beside the perfumed bride and groom,
Daddy would hold me tight against his gray
suit, left hand firmly on my back, the way
I'd seen him dance before, right arm extended,
hand holding hand, my young face inches
from the knot on his tie and white shirt,
leg against leg feeling the beat of the music,
dizzy with excitement, getting it right.

I wanted to dance with my father before
the other women came, leaning against
his shoulder laughing, pressing their distorted
faces against his face. I wanted to dance before
the whiskey bottle made another round of our
table and Daddy's eyes began to shine like
sea gulls lusting after fish and his cheeks
flushed like he'd been standing on the deck
of a ship and he shouted out incomprehensible
Polish words that sounded like "yasha masha."
He would soon take off his tie and jacket,
sweat stains would show under his arms,
and he would smell like vegetable soup.
I wanted to dance with my father, not sit
on a chair next to my mother at the empty
table where my Coca-Cola glass left rings
of water on the white tablecloth.

Grandma Doll

No one buys Grandma dolls
for children to develop their
fine-muscle co-ordination:
false teeth that they could fit in
and remove from a concave
mouth cavity, elastic stockings
that creative children could pull
up from thin ankles, stretch across
blue-veined calves up to just over
the knee, practice for pulling
on mittens before going out
in the cold winter snow.

And then attachments: a digital
television in black and white
or color with very loud volume,
a dial phone with alphabet
clusters for pre-reading skills,
a music box that plays
"The Anniversary Waltz,"
arthritis shoes that look like
big mushrooms—be careful
putting them on, not to crumple
Grandma's crooked toes, cotton
sweaters in patterns that conceal
food dropped at meals and plastic
incontinence undies, look, just
like baby Caroline, transfer of
learning from one situation to
another, then the value sets:
Grandma with metal walker,
Grandma with wheelchair and
an especially installed voice box
that says, "I love you," "I love you."

objects from childhood

There weren't many objects in the room,
no walls filled with leather-bound books
bought in quantity from anonymous eBay
or individually discovered, selected lovingly
at yard-sales across the city, no albums
filled with baseball cards placed showily
on the bottom shelf of the coffee table, "Oh,
yes, this is my baseball card collection," or
flo-blue china dispersed around the walls
in artistic arrangements, meant to catch
the soothing, evening light, rather just
a hollow metal elephant that felt cool
against your cheek whatever the weather
and a pink conch shell that held the ocean.

album

The twins rummage through the dark
clothes closet like collectors at a flea
market, the brown paper bagfuls of old
greeting cards—*Dear Mother on Mother's
Day, From Your Loving Husband on Our
Anniversary, Merry Christmas from
Babushka and Pa*, and through another
bagful of woolen hats and scarves
caressing their mother's old, scratchy,
blue-striped stocking cap that she wore
for ice-skating, she has told them, but
then, unlike other rummages, they find
a strange baby book with their older
sister's name—*Adele* —with a different
last name than theirs. They look at each
other as if they have finally realized
how a magician can find a quarter
behind your ear, and simultaneously
whisper amid the deodorant-pungent
and Coty's Emeraude fragrant clothes
that hang around them: *Adele is adopted!*

Rather than directly ask their older sister
or mother for more information, but, of
course, never their father who responds
to questions with gorilla grunts most of
the time, Betty begins to leave notes around
the tiny apartment behind the butcher: *Adele
is adopted* on the white formica kitchen
table that their Mom and Dad have bought
with some of the early inheritance money
from their father's parents, *Adele is adopted*
on the doily-covered end table in the front
room next to the second-hand horsehair sofa,
Adele is adopted on the woven clothes hamper
in the bathroom.

Finally, their mother says, "We'll have
a little talk after school today." *We* means
Mother and the twins because Adele
at seventeen, is a flirty girl and their Dad
just either naps after work or sits in front
of a Cubs game with a Blatz, so after school
the three congregate around the new table
as they do when they play Clue or Parcheesi.
Mother explains in the oily voice she reserves
for menstruation, old relatives dying or why
they have such an old car, "I was married
to another man before I met your father,
so Adele is your half-sister."

The penny drops into the gumball machine
as Barbara remembers the photo in Grandma's
album of her beautiful younger mother in
a lacy white bridal gown standing next to
a man who is not her father. When she asked
about it, her Mother exchanged a look with
Grandma and said, "I was standing up for
a wedding," but she lied.

Stems

My mother always cut the gladiola stems too short
whenever my dad brought them home. Cradling
the long stems in the crook of his arm, coral or
magenta tissue-thin flowers laying complacently
exposed in crinkly florist wrapping paper, he'd
hold out the gladiolas to her to arrange in a vase,
then she'd grab them away from him with her jerky
movements and slice off half their majesty. Actually,
they were his favorite flowers, not hers. Hers were
cinnamon carnations. But maybe she had some
compulsion to trim things down to size in general.
When Kodak still developed photos with a white
frame around the outside, she would cut that off
without a ruler so all the photos from our youth
are small and have crooked edges except that
photograph of my twin sister and me sitting on bikes
in sun suits in the backyard. That one, at least,
survived the scissors. Just yesterday she told me
that she still cuts cantaloupe in chunks then stores
the pieces in a glass jar in the fridge, never to ripen
naturally in gentle air.

where the water lilies grow

My dad feathers the oars clumsily so he can get
to where the water lilies float on the green silk
surface of Twin Lakes, Wisconsin, neither rowing
nor spending time with us activities he regularly
chooses, but perhaps because he used the "F" word
again with Mother this morning at breakfast, or just
because he's on vacation, some tenderness appears
to permeate his newly sun-tanned skin because he
says, "Let's pick this for your mother," so, almost
over-turning the rowboat, he reaches out and plucks
the pink flower from its quiet habitat among the rushes,
turns the boat back toward the pier and ties it up as
my sister and I clamber ashore unsteadily as drunks.
Exulted that he got something right, my dad walks
thoughtfully along the path in the long, beaten-down
summer grass, even holding our hands, then seeing
his friend, Frank Hayes, his eyebrows lift like bridges
as he describes how he found the water lily, but Frank
frowns unexpectedly; he's been a member of the lodge
for many years, so says, "Marty, don't you know it's
illegal to pick those darn things?" Chagrined, my dad
thrusts the flower into the tall grass as petulantly as our
aging grandmother discards food; later, my sister and I
return, lay on the soft ground, and pluck the petals,
"He loves me, he loves me not," then put the desiccated
pieces in our pockets where my mother will find them
when she washes our clothes and will throw them away.

Ozark Vacation

It must have been Missouri when Dad
drove Aunt Sara's shiny new black
Desoto along a bumpy green, dirt road
and crossed a thin stream as we held
our breath like we did when we passed
a cemetery so the apparent trickle
would be as shallow as it looked then
we crept along a little more to the river
where the sunlight shone in jagged
stained glass slivers, Mom and Dad
actually smiling at each other with
some electric field around them like
Mary and Joseph's halos we saw each
Sunday at church. Dad even opened
our car door bowing like a butler in
an Alfred Hitchcock movie then, still
acting silly, poking Mom in the ribs,
he said, "You two wait here at the shore
while your mother and I walk into
the river to look at some flowers," Mom
in the yellow halter that showed her big
breasts and the red-flowered, wide-legged
shorts she wore instead of a bathing suit.
Dad put his arm around Mom's waist as
they waded into the brown water giggling
like our fifth grade friends. They disappeared
around a thicket, parting the water with their
legs, so surely it nuzzled their hips like
a pony, while my twin and I scraped our toes
through the soft sand and wondered about
our parent's odd behavior. Suddenly, we
heard our mother scream into the green
of the quiet cathedral and both our parents
reappeared racing through the water like
speed boats. "We saw a water moccasin!"
their quivering voices reported. Ozark vacation.

my dad makes polish sausage

My dad seasons his polish sausage with real cloves
of garlic, not the powdered kind my mother stores
beside the stainless steel breadbox in the pantry
with the dried oregano flakes and shakers of chili
and sugared cinnamon. He thrusts his graceful fingers
into the pork mixture as naturally as red-faced George
the butcher with his sausage fingers combines ground
pork and veal for mock chicken legs and with an energy
I rarely see when he is sober, mixing the pork cubes
with his own blend of spices that he later conscientiously
writes down for me in a pretty script: a knob of garlic,
a T of black pepper and a juice glass full of salt
which means a Kraft cheese jar that my parents use
for orange juice made from concentrate as well as
for the muscatel they sip before dinner. Now, my dad
guides pork intestines, not synthetic casings, over
the filling attachment of the gleaming sausage maker
as delicately as a woman might pull up her pantyhose,
and, as my mother, co-operatively for once, turns
the handle of the machine to grind the sausage,
as rhythmically as a hurdy-gurdy, my father forms
the sausage links as pudgy as a baby's arm.

bacon fat

Last night we ate bacon for dinner
and are still alive this blue, hog
butcher of the world morning, both
of us laughing about our mothers'
routines of draining the animal fat
from the meat they cooked for dinner
every night—Australian grass-fed lamb
in Sean's case, A & P pork or veal
in mine, into a little white bowl that
they reserved the fat in to use for
frying dinner the next night-no grape
seed, olive, walnut, corn, canola,
sunflower or safflower oils to choose
from and now our own bowl of bacon
fat left over from last night's pasta
fazool when I substituted bacon
for salt pork, the fat still solidifying
on our stainless steel counter before
we dispose of it in its appropriate
steel garbage receptacle in the most
environmentally friendly method,
not down the toilet as my mother
would have done after she'd reused
the fat twelve times.

landlord

We must have been eleven when we moved
from behind the butcher to Alice's white
clapboard two-flat across Irving Park Road
because our landlord wanted the apartment
we'd lived in since we were born for his son
and daughter-in-law (We'd wondered why
he suddenly relented and put in a white
cupboard sink instead of the old one with
a rorshach rust stain in the porcelain and
exposed pipes underneath) and that was fine
except that Mom now had to walk up two
flights of stairs with the groceries, but then,
in the bedroom below ours, Alice started
having heart attacks, which Mother said
was gas; "Oh, oh," she'd moan during
the night like a saint in religious ecstasy
right under the double bed my twin and I
shared and when she thought our footsteps
were too loud, she'd bang on the kitchen pipes
like a crazy xylophone player which meant
she wanted to have a conference with the four
of us around her red formica kitchen table
when we would just sit without saying anything
as if we were sitting in a funeral parlor, Alice
in a pink satin bed jacket, with rosy cheeks,
her iron gray hair perfumed and styled wearing
the floral nightgown she wore like a lizard skin,

so we moved to Mrs. Schuster's near the Chicago
River even though Jenny and I had to walk a mile
in winter to St. Xavier's High School that we just
started in the old neighborhood, me chanting *Great
green gobs of greasy, grimy gopher guts hanging
on the line to dry* just to annoy my sister but we
had a larger apartment with a real fireplace which,
unfortunately, we never got to use since it was so
drafty that we had to stuff rags up the chimney

all winter to keep the cold from waltzing around
the front room and who wanted to use a fireplace
in summer? Mrs. Schuster thought our footsteps
were too loud, too, especially my dad on the front
steps when he came home late after an Elks
meeting, so she'd poke her head out of her
downstairs apartment door with her hair in curlers
and request in heavily-accented English, "Please
you don't make so much noise?"

Finally, Daddy went to his father and asked
to borrow money to buy the two-flat he'd
found in the old neighborhood: canary yellow
tiled kitchen, three bedrooms, one with wood
paneling, honey colored bookshelves in an alcove
so we could display the encyclopedias Uncle
Ben had given us, even though by then my sister
and I had both found boyfriends in the new
neighborhood so didn't want to leave anymore,
but our Grandpa wanted to charge my dad interest
on high monthly payments that Dad didn't think
he could afford on a lithographer's salary so he
reluctantly asked our other Grandfather who said
in that condescending way, "Marty, I'll buy
the house and you just give me rent." When my
mother's youngest sister came to live downstairs
with her family, my aunt and uncle argued a lot
and sometimes Aunt screamed for my dad,
"Marty, help me," when my drunk uncle
threatened to hit her, (even though they were
both six foot tall and she finally did hit him
knocking him down and scratching his face
with her engagement ring) and we'd huddle
down there like scared puppies when my dad
had a few too many himself, but they never really
complained about any of us being too loud, except
when we'd play Elvis' *Are you lonesome tonight*

at full volume which sounded so good, but they'd
just phone us and request in a friendly voice,
"Please turn the music down," and we did.

Behind the Butcher

She steps cautiously onto the sawdust
floor with a pointed toe like the dancer
she wants to be as she and Mother see
their landlord, John Schneider, behind
the counter in his blood-splattered
white apron and a white cap with
peaks of sweat like mountains over
his steely gray hair. He raises his thick
eyebrows like a bridge but doesn't smile
as his face reddens to the color of calves
liver in the refrigerated counter. She
looks down at the floor to make a pattern
in the sawdust as she senses Mother's
maneuver behind the counter like parking
a jeep in a familiar place on their street.

She has memorized the sliced sweet
pickles, jars of sauerkraut and little
round red beets stacked on shelves
behind her but in front of her, above
the cold rump roast, pig tails and
bratwurst arranged in neat rows, she
can only just see the butcher's hammy
hands encircle each of her mother's
full breasts. Later, after their landlord
wraps the pork chops in smooth white
paper and puts them *on account* and
they are half-way out the glass door,
she turns to ask her mother, "Why did
you let John touch you like that?"
Her mother replies, "You have to notice
everything, don't you!" Despite the sting
of her mother's voice, she pirouettes into
their Chicago gangway toward their
four room apartment behind the butcher.

Mother Drinks Wine on Thanksgiving

Mother, out of the nursing home for Thanksgiving,
skeletally osteo-arthritic at ninety-two, smacks
her thin lips at the first taste of white wine like
Priscilla, Queen of the Wine Harvest; Mother,
who could rival any buxom woman just a few
years ago, reclines concave now in our gray leather
living room, picks a tapenade-stuffed tomato with
her claw-like hands from a plate on her lap, nibbles
the crabmeat from a crouton and smiles encouragingly
as we refill her wine glass, the pale Riesling reflecting
on the ceiling and walls like transparent coins of
backyard honesty.

Once at the table, the ruby red sparkles and Mother
firmly grips her crystal stem like a baby with a new
rattle despite her twisted fingers, and proclaims her
usual toast in her strong, raspy voice before sipping
lustily. Later, we move back to the living room to play
charades, a game you'd think her deafness would
facilitate-signing "the" with her hands, demonstrating
syllables on her forearm, but instead, she lifts the heavy
wine bottle and pours herself more zinfandel.

Dessert served in the dining room again, the chandelier
blazing above the mahogany table, sauterne with the French
apple pie, muscat with the chocolate cake, Mother asks
for more like Oliver, but unlike his abrupt refusal, we kindly
say, "no," not wanting her to fall when she returns to the
nursing home after her last glass of wine on this family day.

rummy

Last week, the urine corridors sting
our nostrils, surround us like prisoners
from an Alexandre Dumas novel;
skeletal women bend over lifeless canes,
never upright on magical moses staffs,
the parting of the waters somewhere
in the inaccessible past, Mother,
the Lysol Queen of our youth, unable
to smell the putrid stench she has
probably contributed to.

But yesterday, we visit en masse
like Chosen People, Joanne, Geoff,
Ron and I in Joseph coats, a melody
shepherdly flutish in our footsteps
even after heavy potato pancakes
for brunch at Sally's local diner,
the halls sanitized presumably after
my call or substantial Sunday staff.
We amble down to the recreation room
at Mother's pace, Joanne greeting the ladies
she sees on her regular visits. One woman
says to Ron, "Hello, Jack," and we laugh.

Arranged around the table for cards,
we pick up, discard, praise and
complain as we always have, Mother
surprisingly taking her turn although
we realize she's hoarding the cards
we need to lay down our three-of-a-kinds,
but now we play like Ya-Ya non-gendered
siblings, exchange looks, smile, positioned
between the old man in the reclining wheelchair
on one side and the almost catatonic woman
on the left, and call out "Rummy!" when
Mother finally releases one of the cards
we've needed for a while.

circus flower

Last night when we ordered red wine
at our favorite Italian restaurant,
the sommelier decanting the Chianti
Classico Reserva said, "You'll find
this wine smells like dead roses,"
and as I inserted my nose below
the rim of the crystal glass to find
out for myself, I suddenly smelled
the fragrance of the plastic rose
my sister brought back from the circus;
more fragrant than the ecclesiastical
incense that used to waft around
our heads on Easter Sunday or
the Evening in Paris my mother
splashed on her underwear before
going out with my father on Saturday
nights and now this wine.

The weekend after my sister brought
the rose home, she took me to the circus
with her where we sat in a canvas tent,
sucking our pink cotton candy. When
the knife-thrower appeared smelling
of straw, sweat and faintly of manure,
he asked for a volunteer. My sister stood
up as confident as a tight-rope walker.
She went to the wall that the knife-thrower
indicated with a nod of his head as relaxed
as if this tent were our living room then
established that placid look on her face
somewhere between boredom and caution
as she locked eyes with the knife-thrower
and pressed her bare shoulders against
the wall while I could only stare dumbfounded.

The knife-thrower thrust his first knife
with his hairy hand and fear leapt between

my shoulders like a horse scared
by a rattlesnake but I had no need
to worry; the knife pierced

the wall cleanly beside my sister's
very round hip. The next glittering blade
slashed the wall beside my sister's right
thigh very close to one of the gray stripes
of her sundress and the third knife cut
the wall next to the other thigh. My mouth
was dry. Later, my sister told me that
the knives were pushed from the other
side of the wall, so the whole act was
a magician's sleight of hand. As we left,
my sister gave me another fragrant rose
which I kept under my nose all the way
home on the bus.

My sister leaves home

and Mr. Bannister stands naked in the window,
so I've heard my mother and aunts whisper
saying, tsk tsk skinny old Mr. Bannister, so
naughty ha-ha so when my sister invites me
to stay overnight I naturally look out the stairway
window on the way up to her part of the house
in the back to see if Mr. Bannister is there
with no clothes on but he isn't.

In her cubby-hole kitchen, my sister has made
chicken salad sandwiches for dinner and she
bought root beer that we drink with striped
straws in front of the television on fold-up
t.v. tables that she takes out of a closet that has
a gray door on the front like an accordion.
After my sister checks that no one is in
the bathroom, she draws a bath for me in
the bathtub that has lion-claw feet like the one
we had behind the butcher which was where
we lived before Mrs. Snyder's who said
we were too noisy just from walking and
when I go in there, it smells like flowers and
has bright lights and I pretend the bubbles
she made for me are snow and pat them on
my body to make a snow bikini top even
though I only have a flat chest yet.

While I'm in the bathroom, my sister makes up
the daybed for me in the tiny living room where
we watched I Love Lucy before I got in the bath.
When I ask, "Where are YOU going to sleep,"
she shows me the big double bed on the sleeping
porch with windows all across the front. It is still
so cold out there that she puts her butter and milk
on a dresser but she assures me, "Don't worry
about me. I put lots of blankets on the bed
so I'll be warm."

burying my sister

this looks like
one of those
skinny poems
for my sister when
I had planned
an expression of
grief as big as a
limestone boulder
like the chunks of rock that the French cut from the Calanque to line the Suez Canal; actually, my sister was a very big woman, almost six feet tall with big size ten feet and at her "heaviest", as my overweight family members prefer to say, she must have weighed around three hundred pounds but she had the heart of a ballerina and a gorgeous operatic voice before she ruined it with cigarettes and alcohol and started singing those sultry songs, like "My Heart Belongs to Daddy" but besides taking me to The New York City Ballet, and rubbing my feet before my own amateur performances, she introduced me to real literature: Anna Karenina, for example, and classical music although the day she died of a general systemic infection plus cirrhosis of the liver, we received a notification in our mailbox that she was suing us because we asked her to pay interest on the five thousand dollars she borrowed from us to go to Rome where she appeared to be walking the streets but, regardless of all that, this summer we carried her ashes along the coastal path near our apartment in the south of France, the white cardboard box sealed for customs purposes (I never realized that cremated remains varied in weight from person to person), the heavy box portable in the same Godiva Chocolate bag her friend delivered her in, saying, "She wanted her ashes to be scattered in the Mediterranean, and I know you go there every year," but I couldn't put her in the tranquil cove just off our balcony where the large, flat stones make music clinking together as the waves recede from them; it is too near, so we decided on a beautiful bay along the hiking trail, out as far as we could walk on the rocks without getting our shoes wet, but it wouldn't have mattered anyway with our New Balance Walkers, and we submerged her in the aqua sea, although I couldn't scatter her because I'd seen movies about cremains; it's not all ashes; it's pieces of bone that look like sliced vertebrae and gristle and I didn't want to see that especially after that scene from The Big Lebowski where Jeff Bridges shakes the ashes of their friend into the wind and they all get their friend in their eyebrows and mustaches; no, that wasn't for me so after we submerged my sister we sat on the rocks and ate the picnic I'd brought, half a bagette each, ham with tomato and lettuce, mayo only on mine, and looked out on the peaceful sea

but I couldn't cry; even

> after five years
> I haven't really
> been able to
> express my grief;
> maybe it will come
> one day when I least
> expect it either like a
> rockslide or thin daily
> filaments of pain.

aunties

the sickly-sweet
deteriorating roses
float in the old,
transparent bowl,
snipped from their stems,
labial and bloated,
petal by petal
fringed in darkness,
glorious and decadent
to the final display

Restless Night

I have not stepped into a chasm getting out
of bed this morning. The vodka hasn't turned
to vinegar overnight, nor has the porcelain
plate I left on the counter cracked, cascading
radishes onto the kitchen floor. I'll drive out
to suburban Evanston to pick up ninety-eight-
year-old Aunt Irene who is bent arthritically
as a bridge over the Chicago River, wedge her
into the front seat of my compact car and pull
the seat belt across her ample Polish bosom
and stomach then take her to see Mother
in her downscale nursing home in the city
helping her to keep her metal walker steady
when she gets out of the car so she doesn't
trip on the frozen gravel path, roll her crunchily
back to my mother's facility in a wheelchair
that I'll borrow from the front desk, then,
after Aunt's certain frustrated communication
trying to talk to Mother who can't hear anything
and doesn't process anything, anyway, drive
around the corner to Wojciechoiwski's Funeral
Home to pay our last respects to cousin Stanley
laying in his satin-lined coffin, as they all do,
a rosary intertwined between his milkman's
fingers. (With any luck, however, his son
Michael's fireman co-workers will be there
with their emergency telephones strapped
to the thin waists that they maintain doing
pushups while they wait for urgent calls to
back the gleaming fire truck out of the firehouse).
I'll drive Aunt back to her senior facility for
her dinner by side streets via a route that I'll plot
on the map I haven't used in years since Mapsearch
will recommend the expressway but I must avoid
that parking lot anytime after 3:15; however,
the snowstorm that the annoying weather person
with the baby voice predicted *hasn't eventuated*

(as my dad used to say) and now the sun is
spreading thick kielbasa fingers across Lake
Michigan already warming the day after a restless
night of zero degrees Fahrenheit when I changed
to that heavier floral Lanz nightgown from
the Vermont Country Store catalogue to keep
warm so slept better after that.

lunch with my 101-year-old aunt

I can smell the medicinal odor of her
gangrenous leg rotting under the white
restaurant tablecloth as she comments
in a loud, deaf voice on various family
members-*litanyesque*-looking up from
her liver and onions for an *Ora Pro Nobis*
response but we merely smile over our
own perfectly boned dover sole with capers
as she tells us that her sister's tenant farmer
in Arkansas is not paying his rent regularly
then relates matter-of-factly that my cousin,
Christina, died, the only one who used to
rescue my sister and me from the slobbery
kisses of my uncles who passed around Jim
Beam downstairs as they watched wrestling
on tv in Chicago's poor Polish Ghetto when
we visited my Polish grandparents as children.
According to my aunt, Christina's alcoholic
brother had his foot surgically removed, too.

I look around for a waiter who might
know the heimlich maneuver in case
Aunt chokes on the bacon slices she is
gobbling from her diminishing lunch,
but I only see a thin young man with
an earring like Johnny Depp wears
in *Pirates of the Caribean* who is pouring
iced water into glasses fogged with moisture
and I can't imagine him squeezing Aunt from
behind until she expectorates the bacon rind
that might get stuck in her throat. Other elderly
people who are scattered around the room like
Las Vegas gamblers lift forkfuls of mashed
potatoes to their lips with Parkinson's hands
or leave red lipstick smudges on strawberry
martinis and next month we will see them
no more.

chagall playground

We float above swings like Chagall
cow and goat helium-filled balloons
in the grass green and fairy floss sky.
Only the clank of metal on metal
chain links and the briny emanations
of iron licking our fingers earthalizes
us. Still not content, we climb above
the tinker-toy jungle gym and march
like toy Russian soldiers in the soft air
above it.

Grandpa appears at the playground
gate in suit, tie and Panama hat and
we deflate. He sits beside Mother
on the park bench and they collude
like Bolsheviks with sen-sen breath.
My twin and I try to equilibrate
unsuccessfully on the teeter totter like
client and painter negotiating a price
for a portrait. She always wins because
she is twice my weight so taunts me
yet again:
   buster, buster, buster brown,
   what will you give me if I let you down.
I say, her favorite, "spearmint leaves",
as usual, so she wiggles up the board
to redistribute her weight so I can finally
put my feet on the ground.

No longer lacking gravity, we shove
each other toward the sandbox like
the basketball players we hear huffing
in a different part of the park. We hear
horseshoes clang in the distance from
where old men are competing.
In the corner of the sandbox, we unearth
squirming maggots with a discarded
popsicle stick and smash them.

pre-teen

It wasn't a made-up childhood game
of one, two, three o'leary or kiss-the-
garage, running from the splintery back
porch safe to the sewer cover and on to
the garage kissing the gray paint
the designated number of times, ritual
in that little square of green between
our building and the alley, while
the dutch elms with their ragged elliptical
leaves were chopped down one by one
and Uncle Ralph's car changed from
a nineteen-fifty two Desoto to a seafoam
green two-tone Ford and he helped to
move our few possessions across
the street to Alice who moaned in distress
most nights in the bedroom beneath ours
because she had a bad heart, she said, but
really, it was probably gas, Mother observed,
and the soft petals of adolescence fell on us
at Alice's like the cherry tree blooming
in the new yard we weren't permitted to use
except to take out the garbage, in our first
spring away from our first home, four rooms
behind the butcher, when Paul Anka sang
Diana and we saw Miss Sadie Thomsen
at the old Northcenter Theater then stood
in front of the cleaners in the rain
wondering if the emotions we felt were
a sin and we never, ever kissed the garage
again.

my father's boxy girl

My father draws the buttons down the front
of the boxy jacket, then sketches the straight
skirt, his face puckered in concentration as if
he were threading a needle in poor light not
clutching a pencil at the fluorescent kitchen table.
Below the skirt he draws vertical lines for the calf
to ankle and shoes that look like horses' hooves
with a little strap over the instep. At five, I titter,
whether with the excitement of having my dad's
complete attention or derision at his boxy girl, so
he, always mercurial anyway, erupts like a faucet
with a broken washer, spraying saliva on me as he
shouts, "I'll never draw anything for you again since
you don't appreciate it," turning me into a blender
with the electricity of his anger, but that was long
ago. Today, I appraise myself before the beveled
mirror in the mahogany French armoire, my sturdy
shape twisting to and fro in the pencil-thin light
of early morning, opening and closing the metal
buttons of my blazer, smoothing my skirt before I
walk into another day, my father's boxy girl.

bad girl

She takes the neat note home,
hands it to her cologned mother
with a sigh and later overhears
them talk together behind their
bedroom door like conspirators—
he never talks to her—she listens,
always listens to the labored
conversations between forkfuls
of fried potatoes and kielbasa
at the dinner table, the arguments
at night, sees the weekend bruises,
listens to the clank of beer bottles
she drops into garbage cans in the alley.

She watches him from the upstairs
window dressed in church clothes:
gray suit, tie, an overcoat and hat,
swaggering to the corner like
a welterweight, his walk her swagger
now that she's older.

The next day at school the Catholic
sister looks her in the eye and says,
"How can a girl like you have such
a wonderful father?" She blinks,
looks down and picks a cuticle.
Bad girl.

fruit basket

In sixth grade when my sister and cousin had
rheumatic arthritis for six weeks, and Ginger cried
every time she got blood drawn at the doctors
but my sister didn't ever, Sister Prisca,

who was a witch, sent Judy Larson, the new girl,
and me to a grocery store far away to buy a basket of
fruit with two dollars in change in our little pockets
(or whatever it cost to buy a basket of fruit then)

that we collected from the other kids in the class
and all the way there the new girl talked and talked
about boys tying girls to a tree in her yard naked
and prodding them in secret places with sticks

then pouring vinegar where they poked and I said,
"Oh, really, oh, really," over and over again,
looking sideways at Judy Larson talking
and talking with her blue eyes wide and her saddle

shoes one after the other on the sidewalk and we
took turns carrying the heavy fruit basket, red apples,
round oranges and walnuts piled up under slippery
cellophane all the way back to school where we gave

it to Sister Prisca who cackled and said, "Good girls
but you took long enough," then after school I came
back for it with that red wagon and Sister Prisca
carried it down the polished marble stairs with her dusty

smell and very wrinkled hands and I pushed backwards
against the brass bar that opened the outside door and
when I pulled it home in the wagon my mother said, "My
stars," but my sister said, "Nobody likes me anyway. Sister

Prisca made them do it," but we ate an orange that we never
had except every couple of weeks segmented for breakfast

and cracked the walnuts with the nutcracker that we used for Thanksgiving even though it was only two hours to dinner.

better than throwing stones

"I can throw a stone as far as you can," I say
to my cousin, Bobby, at puny eight, so I throw
a stone at a little boy's head and as I watch
the blood ooze out of his skull like pancake syrup,
his mother comes out on the front porch, her lips
and forehead puckered like a cabbage patch doll,
and asks me conversationally, "Why did you do
that?" but I can only turn my face away in shame
because I'll never know.

I walk the few doors to my cousin's house where
immediately I am rocking in my favorite auntie's
arms as she cradles me the way she'd hold one of
her regular babies while I sob and sob into her pillow
bosom until I have to leave for dinner at my own
house, so I scrape my yellow keds down the Chicago
alley the half-block home as anxious about my mother's
reaction as if I'd lost her one gold, opal ring, yet still
lulled by my aunt's gentle ministrations.

Just past the pink peonies in the side garden, ants
crawling along their serated petals, I open the screen
door as unobtrusively as possible, but my mother
can see my blotchy cheeks so, stepping aside from
the pork chops she's browning, asks, "What's wrong?"
Eyes rimmed with tears again, I choke out the story
like ejecting a cherry pit half-swallowed, wincing,
half-anticipating the hard slap on my wet cheek I get
accompanied by the shrieked chastisement, "You are
a bad, bad girl."

And I believed her all these years until my daughter
gave me The New York Times best seller: The History
of Love, to read where the protagonist also throws
a stone at another child but his father wisely says,
"You'll find something better than throwing stones,"
and I have.

Mrs. Johnson's Trading Card Collection

All summer we sprawled on the gray porch steps
as confident as Bedouin traders, casually flicking
the rubber bands on our trading cards, pressing
under our nails the smooth corners of the new editions
we'd bought at Flo's Confectionary Store, nudging
the worn playing cards our relatives had found for us
in old buffet drawers; clubs, diamonds, hearts, spades
laminated on the backs of camels, flowers and flamenco
dancers from ancient canasta decks; the air still as a desert
around our pre-teen ears as we negotiated the two or three
cards our opponents-in-trade sometimes begged for one
coveted picture, but then Kathy took me to see Mrs. Johnson's
trading card collection stored in a room as antiseptic
as a hospital, stacks of metal drawers pulled out of a filing
cabinet: a hundred horses prancing, trotting, cantering,
galloping in forests, on hillsides, across race tracks or
standing alone in the home paddock with their heads folded
over the fence. There were flowers embedded in paper weights,
state names in different curly scripts—New Mexico, Alaska,
Hawaii—landscapes, fruit bowls and Fords in metal precision
ready for Mrs. Johnson to take to the Conrad Hilton Trading
Card Convention in downtown Chicago. I walked home slowly
that day, along the leafy street only pausing occasionally
to shuffle through my own small pack, checking to make
sure that my two sleek horses still held their heads high.

Latin Grammar

Crazy Latin with all those q sounds
like qui, quae, quod, cuis, cuis, cuis—
is that the dative?

In English, too, grammatical oddities
abound like how we strangely change
some plurals internally—foot to feet,
mouse to mice , or woman to women—
who decides that?

I tell my E.S.L. students that many
of the irregular forms came from
different families of languages: Anglo-
Saxon, Celtic, German, and were codified
long ago by groups of old didactic men
with long gray beards who met in dusty
libraries and felt superior, like ancient
language police, but actually, all of that
doesn't matter; it's easy enough to find out
where some dipthongs come from (o-u-g-h,
for example). You only have to look in
a History of English Language text where
you can usually find origins of words which
is really like looking in a family album.

For example, you can tell which child was
favored by whoever is holding her in the photo
or who is smiling and looking into the Kodak
camera not down at the ground next to sepia
Mom or Dad. I either read that somewhere
or heard it in a lecture (either/or, of course,
are from Latin Grammar, aut-aut, I still
remember) but who cares who was favored
anyway now that we're literate adults and
nothing can hurt us anymore.

suspended for smoking

Sister Anselma smells the Salem
Menthol on her breath as soon as
she hands the room pass back so
winces like she's stepped in "dog
dirt" (as good Catholic girls used to
call it) then tells her as sternly as
a high school basketball referee,
"Take this note and all your books
to Sister Beatrix's office immediately."

At the office, it's not as bad as she
thought it would be: she waits to see
the principal, (you know how to spell
principal because the principal is your
pal as distinct from *principle* which
is the other one like principle on
money that is lent, *l-e* at the end) and
in this case it's true because Sr. Beatrix
only says, "Diane, we suspended Mark
O'Brien last week for smoking so I'll
have to suspend you, too. Just go home
for the remaining twenty minutes
of the school day and you can walk
over to the convent with your parents
to see me at 5:00, then return to classes
tomorrow."

As soon as her father comes home
from work at four o'clock as regularly
as the St. Benedict church bells, she
approaches him tearfully while he is
in his closet changing out of his red
plaid work shirt. It is his birthday so
Grandma and Aunt Barb are bringing
his favorite lemon meringue pie to have
after dinner, but he says calmly, "We
can fit this in," without the usual sarcasm

that stings like the stripped compound
catalpa tree stems our friends used to
whip each other with as children.
On the other hand, Mother, ordinarily
as comforting as a second blanket on
a cold winter night, screeches like
her pet parakeet, Perry (after Perry
Como), "How could you shame
our family like this, especially on
your father's birthday!" She says:
"I don't know," and she never will.

vocation

She came looking for a sherpa,
wigwam, igloo, anything to enclose
her: glass conservatory with transparent
paneled walls, traditional Japanese paper
barriers or French louvres so they rolled
beige wallpaper over her, locked her
in a closet, dehydrated, deloused,
desensitized, almost decomposed her
after she staggered to their wrought iron
gates blinded like Saint Paul by the voice
she heard on Saturday afternoon praying
the Stations of the Cross, "Follow me,"
rattling the reduced interior reserves
she thought she had to will the energy
to climb stairs, press the doorbell, arrange
her hair in the hallway mirror, walk away
from her parental home for this cocoon
where she will develop wings to fly
or be eaten by predatory insects
in the convent hive.

Chapter of Faults

I'm sorry Sister Gerald Marie, that when Sister Janetta and I tittered behind your tall, broad farmer's back in Theology class Sister Angela thought that it was you being disruptive so she assigned you to collect the re-usable sanitary napkins in the novitiate for penance and everyone looked down at the Terraza floor and held their breath when you passed carrying the bulging pin-striped blue sacks over your quite ample shoulder except Sister Elaine Joan who inhaled for pious self-improvement.

I'm sorry Sister Caroline that I distracted you in the vegetable kitchen while we were chopping carrots and praying the rosary so that you cut off the tip of your little finger and had to spend a week in the infirmary under sedation for the pain but I made the sign of the cross every time I passed the infirmary doors even though Sister Angela wouldn't tell us how you were doing when we asked, or she replied, "Just fine, Sister," with that sneer of sanctity she always had on her pock-marked face. I did rinse the blood off the carrots, just so you know.

I'm sorry Sister Eileen that I initially questioned Dr. Harrison when he suggested that he pull all my top teeth. I should have been more submissive and I know I didn't lay quietly enough in the infirmary when Sister Mary Ann came to check on the bleeding and I wasn't grateful for the cubes of dried bread soaked in milk that she brought me to suck, trying to still make jokes among all those dying sisters around me laying peacefully in metal beds. "Hush, you'll hemorrhage," you said, concerned.

I'm sorry Sister Jude Marie that I didn't dust the pipes under the novitiate sink well enough to make them shine. I admit that I was thinking about the Pardoner's Tale in Chaucer for our test tomorrow and not Thomas Aquinas who we studied in Theology class this morning. I should have known how to do a perfect job the way Saint Therese did cleaning the sores of leprosy patients singing in my head, "As a grain of sand looks longingly toward the mountain/I look toward God," like her, our class's patron saint. I'm sorry Auntie Jean, I'm sorry Lizzy, I'm sorry Mother, I'm sorry Dad.

Convent laundry

Again assigned to work in the convent laundry,
not a prestigious job like cleaning the priest's
quarters, cutting up vegetables in the kitchen,
or counting out patent medicines in the Sanitarium
from requisitions nuns on mission have sent in,
Sister Marie Celeste folds back her black serge
skirt and fastens it with a safety pin so it looks
like a bustle over the red plaid underskirt that
her beloved high school nuns made for her
when she entered the convent a year ago.

After morning instruction, she has walked silently
to the laundry with the other assignees, and has been
given the worst job, sorting the dirty linen from
the San with its peculiar smell of mushrooms and
mud since patients recovering from various emotional
imbalances take long baths in aquatic basement rooms
with chemicals she has smelled when rattling
the canvas laundry wagon through the fallopian
tunnels that connect all parts of the convent, to pick up
the dirty laundry, and now, without protective gloves,
she sorts slimy sheets on one pile almost expecting
to see snails emerge, open-front hospital gowns
on another, bobbing up and down, up and down like
the dickey bird on the rim of a glass that her father
used to bring home from George's tavern in Chicago.

Finally, Sister Elmira screeches her name in heavily
accented German-English and shouts over the clanging
of the machinery, "Marie Celeste, mangle, feeding,"
so she will feed sheets into it that other sisters have
straightened onto long poles that she and her partner
will swing onto the hooks on the side of the machine,
then, grasping the corners delicately, like pinching
a square of toast as she has been instructed to do by
the Novice Mistress, smoothly maneuver the cotton
through thumb and forefinger toward the hot rollers.

Feeding the sheets onto the mangle is a job she likes since
she usually gets to work with Sister Jean Marie who is fun
even though they are forbidden to talk except for praying
the rosary aloud, but they use gestures and occasionally
exchange a verbotin look, definitely not consistent with
the custody of the eyes, until Sister Elmira rings the bell
for lunch where, after Vespers in the convent chapel,
where the novices meekly acknowledge their sinfulness,
they will replenish their strength for more work
in the afternoon until choir practice when they can sing.

Catholic Church in London

I rest my aching traveler's knees
in the last smooth pew of St. Mary's
Moorfields en route to Marks and
Spencers Finsbury Pavement
(as the British quaintly call some
streets) to buy new monochromatic
socks when I am suddenly jolted
by the ritual I knew as well as
my morning routine of orange
juice, oatmeal, decaffeinated tea—
the deep bass voices of two rows
of clerics wearing white albs
with lacy hoods adoring female
parishioners must have crocheted
by hand resonate like Iris Murdoch's
cursed bell originally must have
sounded as they chant *Agnus Dei*
in the Latin my ears have longed
to hear again and then I register
requiem and know this is a funeral
mass.

Once again, I am lured into a fairy
tale hive of flickering candles, myrrh
and organ music buzzing around me
like the unveiling of the Czestochowa
Black Madonna, music chords as
vibrato as the first Raiders of the Lost
Ark sequel beneath the Pankot Palace
or, more germaine, the hypnotic
repetition of the Divine Office I said
five times a day as a Franciscan nun,
intoning, *Oh, God come to my assistance*
at the beginning of each psalm, so,
as the congregation turns toward each
other compassionately for the kiss
of peace, shaking hands or embracing,

I avoid the attempt to communicate
of the woman in the plaid skirt
who briefly catches my eye as if
we're in a poker game: are you in
or are you out?

An African acolyte is the only
young male among the graybeards
(I see their bald scalps horseshoed
with sparce white hair from where
I sit adjacent to the action). A man
in tails who must be the funeral
director, appears to ostentatiously
masticate the host as he walks down
the aisle towards me although we
were indoctrinated to think that all
that jaw action was sacrilegious but
maybe that rule has changed as much
as all the others so now it's quite
alright to chew the angel bread.

After I buy the gray socks and an open-
weave green scarf because I hadn't
chosen well before I packed my travel
wardrobe, I need to rest again so I return
to the fragrant old church. The funeral
is gone but there is more chanting
which I realize is the congregation
reciting the rosary. The leader stresses
you in *blessed are you among women*
in a comical way to my ears but no one
giggles: not the celebrant, not
the kneeling people nor miraculously
the statues—The Infant of Prague
in golden cape, as I remembered,
Mary painted in blue, Joseph across
the aisle supportive of his wife and

child as usual, St. Anthony holding
a baby Jesus, or Jesus, Himself,
exposing His bleeding heart above
red flickering vigil lights, not even me.

The Pope in Dorothy's Magic Shoes

He wears red shoes, so comparisons
with Dorothy seem appropriate. Both
of them iconic, revered, infallible, they
stir audiences to Emerald City expectations,
earlier today, for example, The Stations
of the Cross starting at St. Mary's Cathedral,
attended by the munchkin young congregated
in Sydney for World Youth Week, identifiable
by their orange and yellow backpacks, almost
a costume, and rectangular plastic I.D. tags
located on their chests like a tin man's heart
designating their origins: Mexico, Samoa,
the U.S.—dream destinations for Australian
pilgrims from other parts of Oz, and now
the simulcast Crucifixion across the harbor
from our hotel at the Hungry Mile, purple, red
and white dramatic lights and ecclesiastic music
hanging tonight and all week eerily like menthol
vapor rub between the shores. Technology lifts
the center cross upright with the curly-haired
Jesus actor whose make-up makes him look like
he's been beaten like a victim of police brutality:
he has scrapes and bruises, plus, we see closer
on our t.v., he wears a crown of thorns; I know
the story well from my own Catholic childhood.
I shiver uncontrollably like the straw man
in the face of fire, either from the chilly Sydney
night or some primordial memory.

nosebleed

This is my nosebleed, not yours, although I do appreciate
you trying to assuage my fears by telling me your own
nosebleed story about your knee surgery in Australia
when you were only fifteen; you had a nosebleed while
recovering, so the nurse alerted the doctor as he strutted
through the ward with an entourage of interns in their
green scrubs, nodding and looking thoughtfully down,
the way they do, the surgeon clicking his two hundred
and fifty dollar tasseled loafers on the marble floor-click,
click—I imagine, and even though he saw that your bed was
a bloodbath, according to you, he only said, "Redheads
bleed at the nose," which you seem to think is hilarious
and it obviously had a strong effect on you because you
told me the adage exactly the same as you've been telling
it all these years without changing one detail to apply to my
specific situation and I'm glad I gave you the opportunity
to tell it again but I already know from *Home Remedies* that
you don't have to worry about a nosebleed even if you bleed
for an hour, just keep pinching your nose while you're in an
upright position like gesturing "P.U." and maybe put
an icepack on the back of your neck (or maybe a six-pack,
ha-ha) to constrict the capillaries that are irritated and you can
take Vitamin C and limit aspirin which seems to dilate capillaries
but everyone knows that and you're supposed to try to expel
the blood clot that forms because it interferes with coagulation
like I expectorated this morning which is really what made me
nervous more than anything else seeing that slimy blob ejected
from my body like that alien who popped out of Sigourney
Weaver in the movie, so, as I said, you were able to tell that story
again but now that I feel less anxious I'd like to hear it one more
time because I really wasn't concentrating on what you said
before but I did absorb your comforting tone of voice
which I appreciate, Darling.

Upstate New York Defined

Tonight our didactic waiter in Rosario's
tells us that Rochester is not Upstate New
York but what is upstate if not snow
when our winters there could only have
been more brutal in the Arctic—the snow
accumulating against the garage doors
like fused stalagmites and the adolescents
living with us—our daughter and her red-
haired friend, who we took in when she
told us that her step-father beat her with
a clothes hanger (our daughter had already
called social services), both of the girls
shoveling snow away from the garage
doors with adolescent vigor so we could
hopefully get the Audi out to go to Wegmans
for a prepared chicken as the snow relentlessly
piled half-way up the upstairs windows
like inverted shades, obliterating the pool
house, Karen and Bethany laughing
as joyously as kookaburras, exhilarated
as they shifted shovelfuls of snow into
the red radio flyer wagon then dumped
on the other side of the driveway.

Meanwhile, I holed up in the living room
submerged in Proust in front of the glowing
vermont wood stove never able to understand
the dynamic interactions: the hormone
shoveled snow, the girl we took in who put
her jeans in the drier so they'd be skin tight,
then had to recline on the bed to zip them,
and our daughter who laughed through
all the storms.

Buying Shoes in London

You have just bought a pair of Churches' English
shoes "with branches in Milan, New York and Paris,"
stamped in gold on the insole and I feel privileged
to have been with you, relaxing on comfortable
brown leather chairs while the attentive British
shoeman who could have been a butler in an Alfred
Hitchcock movie first knowledgeably informed you
that you didn't want slip-on loafers because for
someone with pronated feet, they cause the foot
to slide forward and rub against the interior stitching,
so he brought out these beautiful two hundred and forty
dollar shoes which might be kangaroo, he says,
as you suggested. He clutched your heel with index
finger and thumb like it was a big yellow sapphire
then gently slipped on the black leather shoe, pressing
two fingers against your instep as if he were testing
the warmth of a teapot. He glided his thumb across
the bridge of your foot then appeared to caress both
sides of it and finally reined in the laces which he had
so mysteriously crossed and criss-crossed earlier
when he took the shoes out of their crinkly paper
where they had snuggled companionably together
in their rectangular box before you tried them on
and wore them home, clicking your heels all the way.

I Will Touch Flowers

I will touch flowers until you come
not floating water hyacinths with
glossy green leaves and violet blooms
or water lilies succulent in a satin
impressionist pond at pretty evening
but here on Lake Shore Drive, in Chicago,
when the morning light slivers
at the sides of the pleated shades, I will
caress the sessile hairy gladiola trumpets
terrestrial on their green, firm stems,
waiting for your silk return.

seafood allergy: scallops, clams and abalone

Tonight in this fine Chinese Restaurant
in Singapore, as opulent as a Ritz-Carlton
lobby, you unfortunately must upset
the marble harmony to explain your ghastly
allergy to formal waitresses lined up like
trained soldiers in navy blue suits waiting
for our culinary commands. You place
your hand over your heart as if you're
pledging allegiance to the flag then flutter
your fingers rapidly to try to indicate what
happens to your heartbeat if you eat certain
shellfish, then position your hand palm down
across your chest and press slowly toward
the floor like a plunger in a coffee maker
showing how your blood pressure goes
dangerously down if you eat scallops, clams
or abalone but lobster, shrimp and oysters are
all right, and I remember the last time
in Honolulu when the restaurant had to have
substituted scallops for their famous lobster
pot-stickers, even though they wouldn't admit
it, your face suddenly shining with sweat like
an injured marathon runner and you kept asking
me to find a bed, whimpering, "Do you think
they have a bed," in a weakened voice unused
to supplication and you couldn't move your
fingers, like an octopus with frozen tentacles,
but tonight the wait staff understands; I want to
clap my hands with relief, as, first, they place
the pork-stuffed tofu on the clean white
tablecloth, then bring the bok choy gleaming
like emeralds on a white platter and fragrant
chicken smoked in tea leaves, so we can smile,
relaxed, lean back in our embroidered chairs,
chopsticks in hand, and watch the other diners
appreciate the scallops, clams and abalone.

generosity

That's right! I haven't changed my mind
in twenty years and neither have you,
restating your position as precisely as
a presidential debater at lunch today,
hissing in the restaurant in subdued
rattlesnake tones between forkfuls of
underappreciated-due-to-the-emotionally-
charged-situation deep-fried catfish,
baked potato and salad, the basic fact is:
the gardener slept in the pool shower room
beneath our tropical house on stilts *so he'd
be on time in the morning* (what a claim
to fame) and, yes, he was the best gardener
we could find in Brisbane, but he did
mumble to himself (actually, as you are
starting to do) when he pruned the pink,
long-stemmed Queen Elizabeth roses or
when he buried the frilly-necked lizard
that had fallen into the pool (He had to
fish it out with the wire mesh scoop,
as I recall). I was startled when I woke
up in the middle of the night to find it
wasn't you who coughed, nor was the husky
rasp the baby with croup, either, so you went
down to investigate, twirling the broom handle
in front of yourself like a majorette the way
you did when we heard that thud in the house
that turned out to be one of the long case clock
weights crashing to the floor. This time,
however, you found Lawrence *shivering on
the concrete shower room floor, like a prisoner
in solitary confinement with just a tarpaulin
pulled over him*, (but also a whisky bottle
next to him); then, upstairs again, you asked
me if you should take him a blanket. Of course,
I gasped, *You're kidding*, and in the morning
we fired him, so outraged was I, and now that

I want to write about it, instead of giving me
support for the idea, you question my generosity!
Come on!

Before the Wedding in Cuernavaca

Brian is showering then we are all meeting
downstairs next to the poinsettia display
at eleven-fifteen but then it might be eleven-
thirty or we might even be meeting in front
of the *recepcion;* this is Mexico, after all,
and the *mañana* thing doesn't seem to be
a stereotype, we're finding. I'm already
in my usual stretchy black staley gretzinger
wedding dress (as the designer's name looks
on the label that I just confirmed) with
the potato prints all over it that I can wear
my black Australian opal earrings with,
wide gold bracelet and ruby ring (the
Indian relatives will be covered in gold
bangles; I already saw the groom's sister
with a diamond stud in her right nostril).
I'll probably be the only woman among
the stiletto Mexican *señoras* who is wearing
flat shoes that I should have had reheeled
before packing but my hair looks fine
with just the hotel shampoo and conditioner
and I depilated a few days ago unlike
Laura who I noticed at breakfast depilated
her upper lip just this morning.

tiling the condo

We find the showroom on Central
like scouts on a scavenger hunt
and Junior who looks more like
Senior invites us to sit down at
a table that is covered with floor
tile samples including the one we
chose from Casa Bellisima. We
have purchased tile before but not
a porcelain one as refined as
the marble Cleopatra used for
her mausoleum. Junior, caressing
our sample lustfully with thick
fingertips, observes in a respectful
funereal tone, *The tile you selected
is beautiful* which we presume is
why his son-in-law, the contractor,
recommended *mudset* rather than
the cheaper *thinset* method of laying
it, appreciating our excellent taste.

Ron has already internalized the new
vocabulary so jumps out of his swivel
chair to demonstrate to me—something
I have repeatedly asked him not to do
publicly—explaining with great energy,
this time even using accompanying
gestures: running his hand along
the grout to demonstrate that the coarse
tiles on the showroom floor are rectified
but still almost imperceptibly uneven
as can be seen by their *lippage*—the way
they don't meet at the same height—
because it hasn't been laid in the *mudset*
frame that guarantees the tiles' evenness
but costs thousands of dollars more
to install, however, *mudset* is what
people like Angelina Jolie and Brad Pitt
would choose.

Tulip Shell

Today I smell like fish,
not that I've been catching
any . Could there be some
osmosis between my odor
and the big beautiful tulip
shell we found dying
on the beach, its carnivorous
foot protruding like a slug?
We put it in a yellow plastic
bucket on the balcony hoping
a stray heron or sea gull
would come and do the job
that the shell books recommend
to kill it: freeze the shell or boil
it so it dies then we collectors
can display only its colorful
exoskeletal stripes.

Oddly, I'd never registered that
all those fragile shells we'd found:
augers, cockles, murex, once had
slimy animals inside until I saw
the pink visceral mass
of a luminescent penn shell lying
vulnerably outside its hard covering
last week before a predator ate it.

Now, that haunting memory of
the bearded homeless man laying
on the concrete steps in downtown
Sydney, his zipper open—hanging out
like the soft innards of the shellfish
dying on our balcony.

chicken stock

You are in a taxi checking your e-mails
on the way to The Renaissance Hotel
in London so I have finished the chicken
stock you started yesterday, separating
the carcass, carrots, onions and celery
from the liquid with a slotted spoon like
scooping fish with a net out of The Galilee
(as they say in Tel Aviv), which reminds
me of when your student's parents took us
to that restaurant in the Arab Quarter and
we ordered St. Peter fish thinking it was
the French St. Pierre we like so much but
when the waiter brought it, it was not
St. Pierre, less stream-lined, thick as
swordfish and crossed with black grill
lines and the eye looked up at us challenging
us to say, "No, thank you," but we were not
intimidated by a fish, so told the waiter,
"That's not what we ordered," but he replied,
"Oh, yes it is; St. Peter is from The Galilee,"
(our new friends translated), that magical
word from our childhoods when we believed
that Jesus could really walk on water, which
we tried unsuccessfully on puddles after hearing
the story from the nuns, so we ate the fish
even though it wasn't what we thought it was
and enjoyed its drier texture, chatting with
the charming Israelis who brought us to this
restaurant and ordered a wonderful variety
of meso (or whatever that is like rijsttafel
in Amsterdam): humus, cucumbers in yoghurt—
so many ethnic dishes that they covered
the whole table like a huge picnic, and we laughed
when we discovered that she sings in a chorus, like
I do and I know you have to travel like this for work
and anyway I could join you if I didn't choose

to work, myself, but I do miss you and will enjoy
the chicken stock enormously when I mix it with
leeks and potatoes tomorrow to make vichyssoise.

Water Walking

A big piece of salmon on a blue plate,
she floats in the deep end of the pool
in her pink Speedo bathing suit which
stretches tightly across her slippery skin
when two thin women her age clank
the metal gate of the cyclone fence
enclosure. So they don't see her cellulosed
thighs, she changes position. Then, as if
she were an electric beater, she rotates
her legs beneath her rather than behind
since she has heard that water walking
is the best exercise to slim down. As she
approaches the white rope that separates
the shallow from the deep end like a nautical
theme belt, she can only vaguely see
the women near the pool's edge without
her bifocals. Nevertheless, she smiles and
waves, "Nice Day," as she has seen
thin women in the building do, then out of
the corner of her eye, she sees the one
with brown hair sit on the side of the pool
and detach a prosthetic leg from the knee
down as nonchalantly as if she were taking
off her shoes, then lower herself into the water
on strong arms saying, matter-of-factly,
"I swim every day as much as possible."

Your Father's Plums

We canned your father's plums
purple from the garden, safe in their Fowler's glass jars.
They sat on the kitchen windowsill for months
filtering the mild Sydney winter light
then we stored them in the wine cellar and forgot.

Years later (another gentle, sunny day at our house),
your father took a glass of cabernet, unusual for him,
his tapered fingers fluttered like butterflies
on the crystal stem. The children
burst into the room at dusk stained with mulberries
and we laughed heartily. All of us, except your father.

Then,
before the night set in,
your father, who never asked for anything,
asked about the plums, "If you still
have the plums, I'd like some."
We brought them up and pried the metal lid,
took out our best glass bowls, and spooned the plums, a little cream.
Your father ate the plums and softly cried.

You drove your parents home and lingered.
I bathed the children and kissed them goodnight
just one week before your father died.

Lunch at the Bernadotte Café

We don't know his name—Wayne? Buster?
Like a last survivor of the WW II navy,
he is tattooed and greets us in a curt yet
friendly way, saying, "Hi, Guys," with
a scratchy, tough-guy voice as we sit
down at the Bernadotte Café for iced tea,
fried breaded catfish that we hope is from
the Spoon River, slaw and fries, an order
we must raise our voices to make understood
with his declining hearing and the clatter
of cutlery on formica tables. Farmers recline
in plaid shirts and camouflage caps; wives
wear white or tinted permed hair like helmets
on their heads. We hear them order, "The Sirloin,"
and I turn to the two women at the next table
and ask, "It's good, is it?"

We know to choose a table next to the windows
so we can watch the hummingbirds dart purposefully
in front of us between the feeders he has placed
at strategic intervals outside, bucolic but also
military in the precision of the movements
of their sturdy wings, a dizzying speed like soldiers
with guns clicking and unclicking, dashing behind
trees to stalk their opponents, but now the craggy man
almost throws the plastic plates on the table
in front of us, croaking, "Enjoy," as he always does
and we dissect our catfish along its spine, and nibble
fries and slaw as we observe his hummingbirds suck
sugar from the feeders then fly temporarily away.

Note: During WWII, the town of Bernadotte and the surrounding area
were converted to a prisoner of war camp. There is still evidence
of the camp outside the reconstructed town just past the Bernadotte Cafe.

planting cone-flower seeds

I hadn't seen an earthworm in at least
ten years the way we, walking to
St. Benedict's Elementary School
in Chicago, used to first smell iron—
rain or worms we never knew—then
look down to see worms wiggling on
the flat pavement in rainbow puddles
(I always thought they came up
through the cracks, maybe they did)
and later we dissected them in biology
class, the smell of formaldehyde as
unforgettable as pot roast simmering
for Sunday dinner as we studied our
phylum for earthworms: Annelida,
at the dining room table until Mother
called us to set it with the best cutlery.

Now, I kneel uncharacteristically to turn
the crumbly clay that worms have processed
through their digestive systems into sweet,
rich soil beside the farmhouse that we're
renovating and plant the slivered seeds
that Kathy gave me. Again, I see the fat
earthworms wiggling as regularly as black
olives lay inert in a glass bowl at Thanksgiving.
I know that next summer the purple blossoms
will grow petaled in the afternoon shelter
of the red shingled house that radiates
the constant sun in the morning.

Balancing

We are no longer standing on branches
in the bush pear tree, hugging the scratchy
trunk while we disconnect the pearstem
from the twig with thumb and forefinger,
dropping the round fruit like Newton's apple
into the gathering bag, our family under
the cool green umbrella cacooned in shade
against the simmering, cinnamon heat
of an Australian January.

We will never again try to equilibriate
like tightrope walker clowns across
the shiny creekstones through the splintery
farmgate, lugging our cache of golden nuggets,
our shins slippery with sweat, until we hoist
our horde onto the shady verandah then transfer
it to the kitchen table where we sit down
to rehydrate with a cool glass of rainwater
from the collecting tank, otherwise, a pool
for chartreuse frogs; knives and cutting boards
already in place for dissecting the pears,
we quarter the whole with geometric precision,
then scoop out the core with one flick of the wrist
and peel the thin skin and dice, dice, dice,
in preparation for our annual pear jam canning.

Now our family is together again in harsh Chicago,
the ice a brittle skin across the lake in continental
forms of separation—a floe—a vast expanse
of white—a streak of fluid khaki and we, sealed
in our apartment building, one in town from Austin,
dozing in front of the TV, the other pressing iPad
keys methodically, absent from Manhattan but still
networked. We play cards and drink cool wine
among the changing shapes: diamonds, hearts,
clubs, spades.

Jellyfish Sting

Quivering from the jellyfish sting
in the South China Sea, Daddy wraps
you in his arms and we all rush to the
first aid station where attendants dab
vinegar on the sting to relieve the pain
that must feel like tattoo needles all
the way down your leg. I remind you
that you are Australian with my feeble
humor and you finally smile in your
green bathing suit and even pinch
your older brother playfully.

This morning you swim in the New
York City triathlon near the salty
mouth of the Hudson River and are
stung again by jellyfish on your face,
wrist and ankle where your wetsuit
doesn't cover. Rolling over briefly
on your back like a ladybug in the grass
that has missed its landing on a rose,
you repeat what has become your mantra:
"I'm Australian; I can do this."

But, since your adulthood, you tell us
you add: "I've survived my brother's
drug addiction, the break-up of
a five year relationship, conflicts
with parents, friends, colleagues; I can
do this," and rip off your wetsuit, sting
still burning, and jump on your bike
for the next stage of the competition.

parents at the triathlon

Now that we know how to cheer for you,
we can come to other triathlons, find
the swim start at the specified time and
identify your "wave" by its yellow bathing
caps so we can shout encouragement before
you jump into the water then follow you
along the shore like egrets stalking fish as
you try to avoid the poking toes and intrusive
elbows of the other eager swimmers you've
told us about, all of you sleek as Nascars
competing on some zany aqueous speedway,
yelling until our voices fail, "C'mon Carol,"
even though it's hard to see if it's really you,
a face distorted with effort, the identifying
number—7613—they wrote on your arm indelibly
covered by a wetsuit, then, forty-five minutes
later at the swim exit, we squeeze past hundreds
of waiting friends and other parents like hungry
migrating birds desperately looking for horseshoe
crab eggs on a Delaware Bay beach so we can
observe you emerge dripping from the water,
already peeling off your wetsuit like a backstage
costume change as you transition to the bike stage,
yet, you still find time to give us a thumbs up
and only we stand breathless.

I want to hold you thirty years ago

I want to hold you thirty years ago,
your plump short legs dangling
between mine like a soft, gangly
stuffed animal. My arms encircle
you like fragrant meadow daisy
chains as you lay contentedly
across my thigh, neither of us speaking,
my body a wind-cheater for your world;

                    but now,

you are all multi-task and movement:
you call me as you drive home from
an out-of-town meeting with a client
talking a mile a minute as you maneuver
through heavy traffic. Excusing yourself
to take a call on your work cell phone,
I picture you encased in

                    headphones, iPad,
blackberry, computer, GPS

You are triathlon swimmer, runner, biker,
softball player last night at 9, just before
my bedtime. My arms hang at my sides
when I am with you; my fingers clutch
the clasp on my purse clicking it open,
closed, open, closed, annoying you.

The Gumball Ballerina

One summer you came home
and mowed the front lawn
in the shape of Australia.
You trimmed the shrubs hissing,
"Chop, chop, chop; chop, chop, chop,"
wearing that Chicago Bears hat
you used to pull over your ears.
I sat on the couch pretending
to read and pondering,
"Where has the theoretical physics
student gone? Where could
the long-distance runner be hiding,
crouched inside the emaciated body,
under the hat, under the two-tone hair
that explodes from your head?"

Then on Christmas Eve you came
home again from your squat
in Vancouver, "It has lights and
running water; I can read at night,"
you told us proudly. I wanted to stroke
your scraggily beard and put my little finger
on your new eyebrow scar,
but mothers don't possess proprietary rights
at your age. We unwrapped the gifts you'd
put in our stockings, continuing our family ritual.

What can I say? The gumball ballerina is always
in my change purse. In arabesque, it proudly stretches
in the flat spaces between the dimes and quarters.
It brushes my hand as I conduct transactions.
It waits in plastic silhouette and so do I.

Jason with the silver fish

I download the photo of Jason
with the silver fish and see it is
so heavy that his knuckles are white
with the weight of it, one hand tight
on the tail above his left shoulder,
the other lost in the accosting balcony
shadow; his cigarette drips ashes
from between his determined lips,
the sun pink as a healing wound
across the horizon; so unusual
to catch the black drum on his
first cast into the Gulf as children
on the beach and neighbors we
know in adjacent condos glow
with admiration, but just six weeks
ago, we found him curled up like
a moon snail on his couch with track
marks down both arms red as seagull
eyes, passive with Mexican Black Tar,
and then the intervention, the rehab,
at last clean under our family's
supervision at the beach just a little
longer, and now, at dusk, he has waded
into the water, fishing pole in hand,
to coax this silver beauty from the sea.

Orchid House

Their son with depression last year in France,
our son just out of rehab here—our exotic
progeny, we shake our heads and smile, as if
an umpire made a wrong call, when we refer
to but never totally discuss "the boys" as we
wander through The Selby Botanical Gardens
in Sarasota, Florida, aimlessly as the street people
we saw reposition themselves from one shady spot
to another outside under the palm trees, remembering
our romantic illusions when our son was living
alfresco like the characters in Down and out
in Paris and, London, maybe they were snorting
cocaine and injecting heroin, too, the claustrophobic
humidity of the orchid house more consistent with
our friends' Amazon travels than pastel downtown
Sarasota. When our glasses fog in the tropical
atmosphere, we all laugh as if inhaling nitrous oxide.
We read on inconspicuously placed plaques that
orchids grow in thousands of unique forms,
information we absorb like the facts we learned
at rehab parents weekend.

Some orchids have bulbous pistils enclosed
in crimson petalgates while others have
obscenely huge purple parts—female predators
that lure male bees then trap them, we read;
still other tiny blossoms perch harmlessly atop
the rims of green trumpets like mosquitoes
in costumes. The orchids climb, dangle on thin
vines, precariously fold and project like Barnum
and Bailey trapeze artists, diaphanous but hardy.
By contrast, an Inca male sits statued in gray
double dimension, (probably he has coca stored
in his cold cheeks) serenely chained from predators'
curious fingers while water drips methodically as
an IV in detox, the violent beauty of our orchid-
children calmed, finally, in this environment

of engineered moisture where our foreign friends
walk with us again.

Tattoo

Brian had calves tattooed with yellow
and red geometric shapes as many at
rehab were; and above his left wrist
a topless dancer hulas, which I have
hated since I first saw it, but Sara has
always been pristine: the navel ring
perforation in college which, like
a burn scar, has disappeared, and she
kept only one small rose on her shoulder,
which she and her cousin had tattooed
familially in New York City, under
circumstances, which I prefer not
to know, however, so when they ask
us if we'll drive them to a tattoo parlor
to get matching tattoos, we both reply,
with our best parental disdain,
"Absolutely not," without even looking
up from our tomatoes with hummus, but,
not to be deterred, our daughter argues,
"For my Christmas present to Brian this
year, I offered to pay for both of us to get
tattoos that remind us of what he replied
in intervention to the facilitator's question,
'Brian, will you go to rehab?'" She
continues, after a sip of her cranberry juice,
"Brian said, 'Of course,' so we thought
we'd have those two words tattooed on us
as a brother-sister bond." We can barely
chew the last bite of our lunch, so swallow
it with water like gulping down a huge
diabetes pill before we respond simultaneously,
"Of course." En route to the tattoo parlor,
our son with his usual sense of humor restored,
suggests, "I'll tell them to leave enough room
on my skin for another 'f' in case I relapse."

storybook daughter

You call dutifully as Robin Hood tonight
before I go to bed and the world opens
for me like James and the Giant Peach;
where am I alive if not in the jellied
strawberry layer of your mind, your life
to me like Charlie and the Chocolate
Factory, text-messaging me from a Big
Apple taxi on your way home to off
Houston Street (I'll be sure to pronounce
it right next time) an hour later than me
here in Chicago, mothering you forever
despite your life like a children's book
compared with mine, lately more Violet
Crumbling Bar—yes, an Australian allusion
because, after all, you are half Aussie and
therefore half kangaroo and koala, too, ha-ha.

Where are you tomorrow in your Maurice
Sendak wild island dreams, "Oh please don't
go, we love you so," a family refrain from
your adolescence and sometimes now
(even if your father's love can only peter pan
from far London tonight while I am lonely
here, but I'll never complain as usual, ha-ha);
maybe you're lonely too, but know I love
you alligators all around.

Mother-daughter dinner

Out for a mother-daughter dinner in Sarasota, Florida,
we order wine, the Colombia signature salad and an
assortment of tapas, chatting about our recent purchases
in the colorful outdoor mall, your bright red shoes and
my subdued Israeli mahogany sandals, color-coded for
our ages, perhaps; we talk through our glass of white
wine with salad; the tapas arrive, your glass of red in
front of you, but then the waitress pivots wrong and
waterfalls my glass of red all down your Ralph Lauren
shoulder and onto your designer jeans, but we don't
register what happened until the waitress piles white
napkins on your upper body like snow up north and
says, "Oh, no, oh no." You exit quickly and the solo
man at the table next to us exclaims, "My wife never
would have laughed it off," and the man on the other
side says, "I spill things on myself all the time,"
obviously not totally aware of who spilled what, as
my father structured his grammar. You return all
soda-watered down. The waitress brings another glass
of wine. We laugh and tell more stories of embarrassing
moments we've heard about like when the woman at the
candy counter poured butter on my hand instead of my
buttered popcorn then the waitress says, "Your dinner
is for free and send the dry-cleaning bill." You say, "I
shouldn't have tripped her," and we laugh some more
together as we exit the restaurant, taking some matches
with the restaurant logo as a souvenir of the night.

Texas Two-step

I doze on the beige couch back
in our lysol Chicago condo drifting
through 1940's film noire, cigarette
smoke afternoons in the Texas Hill
Country or smoldering fires from
Smitty's Barbecue in Lockhardt
the day after our son's wedding,
my yellow silk scarf still smelling
of charred ribs, brisket and pork sausage
not aware of when daydreams segue
into slumber, sandalwood incense
encircling a death's head vision as
I drift in and out of consciousness
like a H1N1 seriously sick person.

I've read that people who have flirted
with death say that you feel like you're
eerily walking toward a light at the end
of a tunnel like Russell Crowe did
in Gladiator after he killed the Roman
Emperor when he was badly wounded,
himself, but three days ago I was not
stumbling around dazed in the Coliseum
but alive as a racehorse as I danced with
the groom, the metronome of the Texas
Two-Step jack-hammering through
the elbows of my especially-made jacquard
jacket as he guided me: one, two, slide,
slide, one, two, slide, slide, one, two.

wedding shoes

Your designer Jimmy Choo high-heeled
shoes afterwards photographed artistically
arranged in the bifurcation (I didn't know
if spell-check would accept that one)
of the blossoming sapling like a secret
Victorian love letter and even I wore
my best open-toed Italian shoes
to the wedding that I have anticipated
more than being given two thousand dollars
to spend in a Tod's shoe store in Singapore.

Chic friends from New York wear high
cork-soled wedgies and even Dad has
on his Church's oxfords *sold in Paris,*
London and Milan stamped on the inside
sole, but before the photographs or
the reception, you across the green
parkgrass between Dad and me, like
we used to swing you between us
when you were a child, past frisbee
throwers, past a baseball game,
everywhere the fragrance of fresh-cut
grass to where Glenn waits for you
under the oak tree, not wearing
those pointy shoes some young London
lawyers wear today that the Vatican
forbade Christians to wear hundreds
of years ago under threat of excommunication,
but standing patiently beside the celebrant
who officiates in a simple blue blouse,
black skirt and dumpy black loafers.

Once there, I hand you the Jimmy
Choo shoes since you walked barefoot
on the summer grass, and you sling
one strap across your heel and tuck
the slender feet you got from Dad

into the silver straps across your toes
and sparkle when you say, *yes, I do.*

secret

I know you told us not to tell
anyone about your pregnancy
until after the first trimester
and since anyone means friends,
I DO tell strangers: the three-
year-old lagging behind her group
of daycare children, on Michigan
Avenue, for example. I whisper
to her in the mild Chicago spring
air, *My daughter has one of you
in her tummy* and when she
looks at me curiously (or like
a nut my daughter would say),
the daycare worker explains,
the lady said her daughter is
going to have a baby.

Likewise, today on the 151 bus,
as we pass Oak Street Beach,
I offer my senior seat to a young
woman who appears to have
a beach ball under her blue
and white striped T-shirt. She says,
It's ok (probably noticing the brace
supporting my strained Achilles
tendon) then I tell her, too, on
the crowded bus, *My daughter
is pregnant but doesn't want
anyone to know.* She smiles as
she replies, *I'm due in July,
only a month away.*

pregnant pilot

She was our Amelia Earhardt,
another self-assured, female aviator
in a predominantly male world,
and we would refer to her at dinner
parties, as our daughter's friend,
the pilot, studying Basic Aeronautics,
Theory of Instrument Flight and
Multi-engine Theory at flying school
in Georgia as metalsleek as the planes
she later navigated in her crisp white
shirt and pilot's cap while the rest
of us were shopping at Wegmans and
volunteering for literacy training.
Every time we traveled, we imagined
her voice on the airplane's intercom,
a woman's voice, "This is your captain
speaking," even when we flew
internationally, a goal, she told us,
it would require thousands of domestic
flying hours to achieve and now she
is pregnant; the altitude indicator shows
her still flying upright, but, she says, she
feels as though her world is upside down,
like we did, the gyroscope spinning,
not able to calibrate the exact horizon
inside her. She will not disappear the same
way that Amelia did in her aborted equator
flight, strapped into the Lockheed Model 1
0E Electra then swallowed by the ocean or
captured by the Japanese as some would
speculate. She will disappear like us,
another woman grounded in motherhood.

Six-thirty Diners

Six-thirty diners, a long table
of over-seventies women, powdered
and bouffant, blowsy roses violet
and pink-petalled, yak with coral lips;
floral polyester blouses loose
over stretch pants, Este Lauder
and lavender fragrant, bunyon-adapted
hush puppies over beige knee highs,
they sip their cool rob roys and vodka
martinis in the upscale neighborhood
Italian restaurant where garlic bread
smears their lipstick when they bite
into it with unsteady teeth and wafts
of lasagna float around their jingling
earrings as they laugh throatily
at the same witticisms they've heard
for years, very aware that they can
disregard any need for social decorum
as they turn to talk to Irene on one side
and Barbara Jean on the other leaving
lipstick imprints on their cool cocktail
glasses.

Dinner in Bed

They eat in bed again so they can stretch out
in their underwear comfortably after work
while watching The Simpsons on tv; first,
she brings him salad wedging the three
bottles of dressing between his hairy knees,
because he's never sure until the very last
minute if he wants crumbled bleu cheese,
ranch or caesar; any arugula, boston lettuce,
or cucumber that they drop on their stomachs
they adeptly pierce with their forks like
the men who pick up garbage in the park
with pointed sticks, barely needing to take
their eyes off the tv for two seconds.

Smelling that the spaghetti sauce is ready,
she slides her legs over the mattress while
balancing the salad plates to take back
to the kitchen; unfortunately, a fork slides
off a plate but only leaves a small caesar
stain on the beige carpet next to the star
from coffee last week. Minutes later she
is back in the bedroom with bowls of
spaghetti and meat sauce. She hands him his
and again wedges the parmesan cheese shaker
between his knees because he knows exactly
how much he wants, oops, spilled a little
on her side while laughing at Homer, and
she maneuvers herself back onto the bed
reversing as if she's parallel parking her
Toyota Camry and is soon slurping spaghetti,
head bent down, bowl held up to just beneath
her chin, still able to reach over to the maple
side table for her wineglass, oops, a splash
of red wine on the pillowcase, then Ben
and Jerry's Chunky Monkey before falling
asleep in front of the flickering tv screen.

Eating Police

They are the eating police, of all our friends,
and we are going to Bambino's Italian Restaurant
in Chicago for dinner with them tonight. I am
prepared for them to tap their nightsticks
on the table and enunciate patiently, "No, no, not
the mussels in cream sauce for an appetizer, but
the house salad with oil and vinegar," and I'll
order the grilled sea bass with lemon, terrified
of their reaction if I ask for what I really crave,
eggplant parmesan, which I know is "soaked
in olive oil" due to the bread crumbs absorbing
the frying oil and "topped with greasy mozzarella
cheese" but so delicious, just this once. We will
use no additional salt, of course, and, if anything,
order sorbet for dessert, definitely avoiding
tiramisu and profiteroles not only because they
are inauthentic on an Italian menu. How can
I disappoint my dear old friends who have worked
so hard to assure that their police uniforms fit
smoothly over their flat stomachs and thin hips,
swimming regularly in pools both in Chicago
and Naples, Florida, and tonight their badges shine
like stars eclipsing the mere muted candle glow
on the restaurant table.

Irish Blessing for a Tenor

The road has risen up to meet Pauline,
the wind no longer at her back. Sweet
Adelines plan to serenade her thin corpse
at McMahon's agreeable Funeral Home on
Valentines Day as she lies unsinging in her
casket, vocal cords cottoned against possible
reverberation from a non-intrusive portable
organ set up in parlor nine. I saw the fear
on the elderly singers' sagging heart-shaped
faces when our musical director asked who
would honor the family's request that we sing a
last farewell for her. I know that, like the lyrics,
some tenors believe that an immaculate divinity
will hold them in the palm of his hand until we
all meet again. As for me, no puckered white
satin coffin lining can shelter me from
the a cappella truth: a heartless, existential,
basso-profundo termination.

lunch with Ruth

I saw you glance at the No Smoking sign
at lunch today while I was talking. Only
a second passed while your blue eyes
flitted to the wall, but I saw you. In that
almost imperceptible sideways flick of
the eyes, I thought, "Oh, maybe I've missed
something, a poster of the Aegean Sea or a
catchy quote;" we weren't seated by a window
to be distracted by a passing bicycle or pedestrian,
just sandwiched up against a wall; but, no,
it was only a *No Smoking* sign.

beach scene

Ken died suddenly three weeks ago—
a massive heart attack—after Chicago
Lyric's flamboyant *Magic Flute,*
the first of our high school friends
to go, and here we are on our balcony
in Florida looking down on the purple
gulf to lull ourselves into absorbing
mortality as the sea does, when we see
three teenagers try to beat the waves
while the sun layers
                    the sky
                            like Sedona.

The adolescents in **silhouette** finally
leave the beach wrapped in soft towels
by their solicitous aunts and uncles
gathered for a family reunion their
elders told us about at The Lazy Lobster
last week. I think of Ken's wife,
my friend, mourning as the snow falls
inside the deer-proof fence they just
constructed around their backyard
last summer and we mourn here, too:

   that pink open wound
        on the horizon
             discoloring our chardonnay.

carwash

Liz in the carwash, giddy with the excitement
of first experience, long, gangly spiderlegs
tucked beneath the dashboard, spiky head
almost grazing the sunroof of the Audi Quatro,
claps her huge hands and giggles like
a middle-schooler as the felt straps lash
against the carbody like a giant squid, she says,
then as the car jerks forward, languidly caress
the roof to hang in impotence across the wind-
shield. Next, the whirling brushes with bristles
like a beard, scrape along the smooth doors
and sidewindows but only momentarily before
a sprayfoam across the glass obliterates
her vision and she gasps with open mouth
until a sweet aroma permeates the inside of the
car relaxing her. At last the sign outside blinks
"Carouba Wax" with plastic flames pulsating
and jets of viscous liquid like squidink spurt
across the hood and she remembers.

the second time

You are not the token Jew in book group
any more than you're the token tennis
player or token resident of Evanston
although I have appreciated your Jewish
perspective when we read both *Augie March*
and *The Pianist* but especially when you
matter-of-factly told me that the co-op high
rise building where I live on Lake Shore
Drive in Chicago didn't admit Jews when
you and your husband were looking for
a condo, which would have been the same
time that my dad was taking us for rides
downtown along Lake Michigan on Saturday
night to look at where the "rich Jews" lived
when really it was where the Catholics and
Protestants lived and all this time I believed him
which goes to show you never know about people
'til you get to know them, as he also said, but
he was right the second time.

veiled student

When I first see her in my classroom,
I recoil slightly as I did last week when
I saw the amputated-leg-man on the bus,
his trousers rolled up on one side as if
he were going fishing not protecting
his pants from a snowdrift, and now
I call the roll: *Juan Medilla, Seung Kim,*
Laetifa Al Kaabi and the veiled woman
responds in a loud, clear voice as the other,
unveiled students have, *Here, from Saudi*
Arabia. I like to swim.

The next day I give a vocabulary exercise
in which I ask the students to emote the word,
shock. Piphat contorts his mouth into an O
like blowing bubbles and widens his eyes.
Naschelli inhales then grimaces like she has
eaten too many chilis. *What will Laetifa do?*
I ponder. She raises her eyebrows like bridges
above the green naqib she is wearing today
and twists her neck to the side like the painting
of St. Sebastian with arrows piercing his white
body that I saw at the Prado last year.

In each class, Laetifa volunteers answers
through colorful pieces of cloth stretched
across her face outlining the tip of her nose
which I have become aware of. I accommodate
her wish to not have a male partner for peer-
evaluation of essays. She writes in her journal
how much she enjoys her English classes as
well as eating pizza in Chicago but I can't
imagine how she can eat with the veil covering
her mouth. Last Tuesday, I walk into the ladies
room before class as she is exiting. She backs
up then asks, *Would you like to see my face?*
I say, *yes.*

Joaquin Says Mass the First Time in English

Accustomed to vowels that hover
on the aspirated language waves
of Andalucia, he nervously rolls
the English gravel around his mouth,
clicks the harsh consonant endings
against his front teeth then skips
the *d* and *t* sounds like stones
across the lake of his congregation,
The Lord be with you.

Lamb of God who takes away the sins
of *the world* causes him to lose the final
s on *takes* but the assembled community
so loves this humble, bearded man
who self-describes his poor hands and
poor life bringing them the body
and blood of their Christ that they are
not bothered by his poor English.

The final *Peace be with you,* almost
right, as the participants take hands
in friendship; the *p* and *b* ripple
the same in both languages, so he only
mispronounces the vowel *i* in *with*
articulating it the Spanish way to rhyme
with *heath,* but overcome with such delight
at his accomplishment, he floats out of
the sanctuary relieved, no longer worried
about getting the words perfectly correct.

ADDITIONAL ACKNOWLEDGMENTS

Chapter of Faults, *The Blind Man's Rainbow*
Convent Laundry, *Chapter of Faults*, author chapbook
Catholic Church in London, *Chapter of Faults*, author chapbook
The Pope in Dorothy's Magic Shoes, *Mad Poet's Review*
nosebleed, *Lullwater Review*
upstate new york defined, *Indiana Voice Journal*
buying shoes in London, *Nimrod*
I Will Touch Flowers, *Art Times*
seafood allergy: scallops, clams and abalone, *Karamu*
generosity, *Willow Review*
Before the Wedding in Cuernavaca, *Courtship of Winds*
tulip shell, *Midwest Quarterly*
Water Walking, *Plainsongs*
Your Father's Plums, *Pegasus Review*
Lunch at the Bernadotte Café, *Miller's Pond*
planting cone flower seeds, *The Sacred Cow*
balancing, *Skylines* (Anthology of the Poet's Club of Chicago)
Jellyfish Sting, *Sandy River Review*
parents at the triathlon, *Sport Literate,*
The Gumball Ballerina, *Slipstream*
Jason with the silver fish, *Poetry Bay*
Orchid House, *The Sow's Ear*
Mother-daughter dinner, *Third Wednesday*
secret, *Peregrine*
pregnant pilot, *Voices from the High Country*
Six-thirty Diners, *Connecticut Review*
Dinner in Bed, *Green Hills Literary Lantern*
eating police, *Chaffin Journal*
Irish Blessing for a Tenor, *Art Times*
Lunch with Ruth, *Poppy Road Review*
carwash, Descant, *Fort Worth* (Betsy Colquitt Prize)
the second time, *Atlanta Review*
Veiled Student, *Oyster River Pages*
Joaquin Says Mass the First Time in English, *California Quarterly*

Jan started seriously writing poetry and submitting it for publication in 1998. Since then, she has had 244 poems accepted or published in the U.S., Canada, India and England (hopefully Australia soon). Published poems have appeared in: *Calyx, Chiron, Connecticut Review, Main Street Rag, Nimrod, Phoebe* and many other journals. Her poem, "my face emerges from my face," was second runner-up in the spring 2010 contest issue of *So to Speak*. In another contest, her poem, "carwash," won the 2011 Betsy Colquitt Award for the best poem in a current issue of *Descant, Fort Worth*. Her two chapbooks, *Accompanying Spouse* (2011) and *Chapter of Faults* (2014), have both been published by Finishing Line Press. She is a member of The Poetry Club of Chicago. Besides her poetry publications, Jan wrote a doctoral dissertation at the University of Rochester in 1996. The title is: *Age and Natural Order in Second Language Acquisition. I Wanted to Dance with My Father* is Jan's first full length poetry publication.

Jan taught ESL at DePaul University in Chicago until recently. She lived in Australia for fifteen years with her Australian husband, Ray Ball. Her two children, Geoffrey and Quentin, were born in Brisbane. She is a twin to Jean Helmken and she was a Franciscan nun for seven years (Sister Jeanclare). When not writing poetry, working with her personal trainer at FFC, going to book group or traveling, Jan and her husband like to cook for friends. These background experiences infuse her poetry.

www.ingramcontent.com/pod-product-compliance
Lightning Source LLC
Chambersburg PA
CBHW021152090426
42740CB00008B/1062